Can Yaz Fix It?

By Debbie Croft

Dad was in his van.

"Run and get Yaz," said Dad.
"Yaz can fix the van."

"Can you fix my van, Yaz?"
Dad said.

Yaz got her big box.

"Let me look," said Yaz.

"I can see," said Yaz.

"Yes, I can fix it!"

Yaz got Dad's van to go!

"Yes!" said Dad.

"We can go!"

We got in Dad's van.

"Yaz did a top job!"
said Dad.

CHECKING FOR MEANING

1. Who did Dad get to fix his van? *(Literal)*

2. What did Yaz bring with her to fix the van? *(Literal)*

3. How did Yaz know she could fix Dad's van? *(Inferential)*

EXTENDING VOCABULARY

fix	What does *fix* mean in this text? Can you think of other meanings of this word and use them in a sentence?
box	What is a *box*? What is a box used for? What is another word that has a similar meaning to *box*? If you take away the *b*, what other letter can you put at the start to make a new word?
Yes	What are the sounds in this word? What does the word mean? What is the opposite of *yes*? Ask students to share some other pairs of words that are opposite in meaning, e.g. day – night; big – little; on – off.

MOVING BEYOND THE TEXT

1. Can you tell about a time when your car or van broke down? What happened? How did you get it fixed? Who fixed it?

2. What do you think Yaz had in her box? What are the names of some of these tools?

3. Where do you think Dad and the girl were going when the van wouldn't go?

4. What did Dad mean when he said Yaz did a *top job*? Have you ever been told you did a *top job*?

SPEED SOUNDS

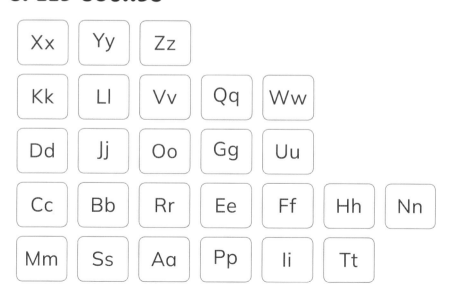

Xx	Yy	Zz		
Kk	Ll	Vv	Qq	Ww
Dd	Jj	Oo	Gg	Uu
Cc	Bb	Rr	Ee	Ff	Hh	Nn
Mm	Ss	Aa	Pp	Ii	Tt

PRACTICE WORDS

Yaz

yet

fix

box

Yes